May you always know how special you are.
A one-of-a-kind masterpiece, filled with
talents and gifts that, when used,
make the world a better place.

This book is dedicated to Caitlin, Connor and Max,
my one-of-a-kind master pieces.
It is an honour and a joy being your mom.

Scan the QR code to listen to the story.

"It's wonderful that the book dives into the fascinating world of animal groups and highlights their uniqueness. Learning about different animals and their special qualities can be so enriching. The book emphasises life lessons, reminding us to embrace our individual strengths and celebrate what makes us special. I absolutely love owls and it's fantastic that this book deepened my appreciation for them even more. What an amazing way to explore and learn about the incredible diversity of wildlife." – **CAROL OFORI** (Author, radio & TV personality)

© Publication: Struik Children, an imprint of Penguin Random House South Africa (Pty) Ltd
The Estuaries No 4, Oxbow Crescent, Century Avenue, Century City, 7441 PO Box 1144
Cape Town, 8000
www.penguinrandomhouse.co.za

© Text: Roslynne Toerien 2024
© Illustrations and design: Julie Smith-Belton 2024

Publisher: Nandi Lessing-Venter
Proofread by: Glenda Laity

Printed by: RR Donnelley Asia Printing Solutions Limited

First edition 2024

ISBN 978 0 6370 0642 2 (print)
ISBN 978 0 6370 0643 9 (e-book)

Written by **Roslynne Toerien**

The SPEEDY SIX OLYMPICS

Illustrated by **Julie Smith-Belton**

I've often wondered about **animals with speed**. Which one would surge ahead and take the **lead**?

Think the **animal Olympics** out in the **WILD**, not for humans, similar, but **restyled**. Each type of animal races heat by heat, to find out which of the others they would defeat.

Fast forward to the finals, the rules **crisp and clear**, only
the **speediest** of each animal could enter and persevere.
It wouldn't matter if they could **run** or **fly**, only the
quickest of each creature could apply.
Then all together in one long line, which animal would lead
and the others outshine?

All of the animals appeared in support, ready to watch this incredibly **wild** Olympic sport:

The **elephant parade** trumpeted in, **eager** for the final race to **begin**.

A THUNDERING

crash of rhinos stormed in together,
not deterred by the very hot weather.

The sneaky **spotted hyenas** arrived as a **clan**, huddling to discuss a **cunning plan.**

A **tower of giraffe** with their necks in the air, and the **zebras** looking dashing with their black-and-white flair.

The **springbok** and **tsessebe herds** gathered with glee, the end of the race is what they wanted to see.

Naturally, without doubt
the **falcons** and **fish eagles**
had the best view, as they looked
out in excitement over the rest of the crew.

The **wild dogs** came out from their
place of hiding, thinking:

"This race is going to be somewhat exciting!"

A **coalition of cheetah** gathered by a tree,
whilst a **leap of leopards** galloped in excitedly.

The **impala nursery** stuck close together, hoping their fastest impala's pace would get better and better.

A lone **blue wildebeest** wandered around anxious and restless, his nerves had him feeling somewhat zestless.

The **ostriches** huddled together as a **herd**, while they fluffed out their feathers, looking rather absurd.

The **lion's** mighty

ROAR

echoed across the reserve,

making sure he was still **KING**

and could be **heard**.

Now, the **tortoise** may have lost in the very first heat, but now was his chance to sound the horn and watch the fastest compete:
This would be a race at a very fast pace,
any form of cheating would be a

disgrace.

Then -

On your marks...

Get set...

Go!

The official horn sounded with a **BELLOWING BLOW.**

The **rhino** charged off leaving a trail of dust,
to him **taking first place** was an absolute must.

The **peregrine falcon** zoomed past in a **whizz**,
leaving the **fish eagle** gasping, all in a **tizz**.

The **blue wildebeest**, although quite slow to the start, had **perseverance**, a **strong will** and **high hopes** for the others to outsmart.

The **leopard**, determined as can be, wished the race had an **obstacle** which required one to climb a tree.

The **lion,** majestic and full of power, raced ahead at **80 kilometres an hour**. With so many animals all around, they still had high hopes that they would be **crowned**.

The **springbok** at **88.5 kilometres an hour**,
raced off agile and quick,
jumping high over obstacles, his favourite trick!

The **tsessebe,** moving at **90 kilometres an hour**,
was racing at his **maximum power**.

The **hyena's** speed was slightly lower,
racing at **60 kilometres an hour**, his pace getting slower.

And running ahead at a **blistering pace**,
was the **cheetah,** not even going all red in the face.

Then everything started to turn

UPSIDE-DOWN

as one thing after the next turned their **smiles** into a **frown**.

What a **disaster**, all the planning **undone**,
as Nature got in the way as the animals started to run.

The **leopard** was not happy with the start time of the race, as a **nocturnal** animal, evening was when he had his speediest pace.

A **tortoise** slowly crossing the road,
a **dung beetle** carrying his
extra load.

Sidestepping these slow animals
in the way,

were the **zebra** and **impala** trying to avoid this
frustrating delay.

The **ostrich** tumbled into the **hyena's** leaf-covered hole,
as more obstacles took a hefty toll.

The **fish eagle** cried
"Oh, that is so
unfair,
he just stepped into the hyena's snare!"

"Quite right, **unfair!**"
a **rhino** retorted,
"We cannot leave this
unreported!"

The **elephant**
trumpeted,
"Stop
the race,
that cheetah **cheated**
and sped off
at too fast a pace."

The **giraffe** tripped, blinded by the sun,
his chance of winning was now
closer to **none.**

Then the **wild dog**,
at **70 kilometres an hour**, was
rapidly completing the final loop,
when...

Oops

he got stuck in the
elephant's
poop.

The **blue wildebeest** racing at **80 kilometres an hour**
full blast, stumbled over thorny branches and his chance to
win passed.

The **springbok** complained,
**"Just look at them up there,
no land obstructions, how is flying fair?"**

Then up in the air, as if not a care,
the **fish eagle** and **peregrine falcon** squawked,
"Of course this is fair!"

The **tsessebe** herd shouted,

"We demand a re-run, with cheating and obstructions, this simply is not fun!"

"Oh please," the **leopard** snorted,
"Nature is Nature, there are no more races later."

Whilst all the wild animals complained about the race,
the cheetah, with focus, sped ahead to claim first place.

Then up overhead, a flash in the sky,
the **falcon**, then **eagle** flew up high.

**"How did that happen, so awfully quick?
I'm not used to losing, I thought I was slick!"**

The **eagle**, distracted by a glimmer in the **river**,
swooped down to catch a fish with an excited **quiver**.

Without thinking, he quickly **reacted**,
a hard lesson in not getting **distracted**.

Diving down cost him
a chance at the crown,
defeated he sulked
and had one massive
meltdown.

"I have an idea," said the tortoise on the ground.
**"We will have two categories of winners to be crowned.
The speediest by flight and the speediest on land,
both have speeds that are very grand!"**

As the **undisputed land-speed record king**,
the **cheetah** then gained courage and started to sing.

"I'm the **fastest land animal** they have ever seen,
the quickest of the cats, a real running machine.
I can gallop, I can run, whilst still having fun,
taking **first place**, coming in at **number one**."

Then following on from the **cheetah's** song,
came the sound of the **falcon** who was very strong.

"I'm the **swiftest bird up in the sky**, just watch as I take
the lead when I fly. **Soaring up high above the rest**,
I really am proud of becoming the best!
Spreading my wings is my superpower, flying at a nifty
speed exceeding 380 kilometres an hour."

Then down below all the animals gathered,
some of them looking rather **frazzled.**
With the **falcon** and **cheetah**, sharing **first place**,
the rest of the top six completed the race.

The **tsessebe**, in **second**, the **springbok** in **third**,
despite all the obstacles that had occurred.

The **lion** claimed **fourth place**, with the **blue wildebeest**
and **impala**, **fifth** and **sixth**,
the rest of the animals left behind in a mix.

Said the **hyena** to the **giraffe**,
"Well, we can **laugh**, you were
asked for your **autograph!**"

The **giraffe** scoffed back, **"You are a nasty pack,
why do you have to give others so much flack?"**

The **springbok** and **impala** appearing shy,
gasped in dismay at the bird in the sky.
"You may be smaller, but wow, you are quick, we would really like to know your flying trick."

The **ostriches** grunted as
they started to compare,
"We can't fly, life is so unfair!"

The **elephant** raised her trunk
in the air, **trumpeting loudly** and
causing the animals to stare:

**"Not the fastest today, well that is OK,
just watch me on another day."**

The **rhino** charged off acting rather **crazy**,

"Don't for one minute think I was being

lazy!"

The **wild dogs** regathered back as a pack.

"We will up our game and come back to **attack!**"

The **blue wildebeest** then stamped his feet in defeat:
**"Today was not my winning day,
let's head out to the trees and rather play."**

The **zebra** looked down,
defeated in despair.
**"I gave it my all,
I'm just happy I didn't fall."**

**"NOTHING
can stop us,"**
a **pride of lions** roared.
Meanwhile, the **tsessebe herd** stomped off feeling ignored.

Then up from a tree, a sharp **hoot** could be heard,
and all of the animals turned to look at the bird.

Said the wise **owl** to the others as she puffed out her chest:

"Please do not be so upset!
You each have a gift which is different to the other,
so stop comparing yourself to another!"

They watched in dismay as she turned her head right around, to them this was really quite profound!
The **owl** then continued with her speech full of wisdom, speaking sense and truth to the animal kingdom.

"Whilst speed may not be your number one thing, there are many other gifts and talents that you each bring."

Then all of the animals stopped looking down
and no longer did they have a frown.
The **owl** then said: **"Let me make this very clear, now is the time for us to cheer. Let's be happy for the cheetah and falcon in first place, at such a fast pace, they deserved to win the race!"**

As they **celebrated** each other, every **talent** and **gift**,
all of their fears then started to lift.

The intelligent **owl** gave the final word,
hoping that she would still be heard.

"Life would be boring if we were all the same,
to be different to each other should not bring shame!
Just look at us all, not a boring crew,
each of us bringing something new."

The animals then looked to the left and the right,
unique in their differences, their **future bright!**

Did you Know?

*Can you spot the hidden **ox pecker** birds in the book?

(Clue: They prefer herbivores.)

Each animal species has its own collective group name.

Cheetahs: A coalition
Eagles: A convocation
Elephants: A parade
Falcons: A cast or kettle
Giraffes: A tower / journey (when in motion)
Hyenas: A clan / cackle
Impala: A nursery / herd
Leopards: A leap (when in motion)
Lions: A pride
Ostrich: A flock
Owls: A parliament / congress or wisdom
Rhino: A crash
Springbok: A herd
Tsessebe: A herd
Wild Dogs: A pack
Wildebeest: A confusion (especially during migrations)
Zebras: A dazzle /crossing / zeal or herd

TOP SPEEDS

Peregrine Falcon: 389 km/h
Fish Eagle: 161 km/h
Cheetah: 120 km/h
Common Tsessebe: 90 km/h
Springbok: 88.5 km/h
Lion: 81 km/h
Impala: 80 km/h
Blue Wildebeest: 80 km/h

SPEEDS

Antelope:	80 km/h
African Wild Dog:	71 km/h
Zebra:	70 km/h
Ostrich:	70 km/h
Leopard:	64 km/h
Hyena:	60 km/h
Giraffe:	60 km/h
Buffalo:	56 km/h
Warthog:	55 km/h
Black Rhino:	55 km/h
White Rhino:	50 km/h
Elephant:	40 km/h
Hippo:	30 km/h
Jackal:	16 km/h

Meet the Author

Roslynne Toerien

Roslynne Toerien is a proudly South African mother of three children, residing in Durban, KwaZulu-Natal. She holds a Bachelor of Education and has a love for teaching, writing and dance.

Ros is the CEO and Founder of the South African Non-Profit Trust, The LEARN Project which stands for 'Let's Educate A Rainbow Nation' and aims to equip disadvantaged schools with libraries and book corners. Ros has been a guest speaker at a number of events and schools and was awarded The Paul Harris Fellows Award by the Rotary Foundation of Rotary International.

She lives by the motto 'Small actions lead to big change' and this can be seen in the number of school LEARN library doors that have been opened and minds that have been unlocked through the power of books and literacy.

Meet the Illustrator

Julie Smith-Belton

Julie Smith-Belton is a visual artist working in painting, ceramic sculpture, photography, illustration and graphic design.
Whimsy, quirky humour and playful creativity are the themes that run throughout her work.

Julie was born and raised in South Africa and currently lives in Denmark with her family. She studied fine art and graphic design, graduating cum laude. Julie has exhibited and sold original artworks, taught art to children and worked on a number of illustrated short stories and books.

She is a mom of 4 who loves to work on things that bring joy to others and lives with a dream of making everything around her beautiful and of impacting the world through creativity and love.

Other titles by the same author and illustrator:

Under the Baobab Tree

On a hot summer's day, the animals wandered, they roamed and explored, they galloped and soared, in search for the perfect tree for their needs. Many trees were breaking, one by one, from the force and destruction of what the elephants had done.
And looking more closely at the top of the trees, sat fish eagles in waiting to soar and fly free.

Will the animals find the perfect tree?

ISBN 978 1 7763 5771 0 (print)
ISBN 978 1 7763 5772 7 (e-book)

The Rumbling Rhino

This book hopes to create awareness around endangered animals, to help educate and empower the next generation to be the game changers. Who knows? Some readers may even aspire to become game rangers!

It is time to stand up and say, 'enough is enough', even though the task may seem very tough. It is not too late to join in the quest. Let's stand up and put these poachers to the test. There is power in team work as more can be done. Let's stand together to save every last one!

ISBN 978 17763 5769 7 (print)
ISBN 978 17763 5770 3 (e-book)

The Forgotten Four

Join some young explorers on an exciting African Safari, as they encounter the famed big five and extend their interest to the lesser mentioned 'Forgotten Four'. Packed with interesting facts about African wildlife, get ready to join them on a game drive adventure to remember, as they discover just how amazing and vast the wildlife is.

ISBN 978 0637 00644 6 (print)
ISBN 978 0637 00645 3 (e-book)